IMPERIAL WAR
MUSEUM

Daily Life In A

WARTIME HOUSE

Laura Wilson

First published in Great Britain in 1995
by Hamlyn Children's Books
an imprint of Reed Children's Books,
Michelin House, 81 Fulham Road, London SW3 6RB
and Auckland, Melbourne, Singapore and Toronto.
This paperback edition published in 1996 by
Heinemann Publishers (Oxford) Ltd,
Halley Court, Jordan Hill, Oxford OX2 8EJ

MADRID ATHENS PARIS
FLORENCE PRAGUE WARSAW
PORTSMOUTH NH CHICAGO SAO PAULO
SINGAPORE TOKYO MELBOURNE AUCKLAND
IBADAN GABORONE JOHANNESBURG

Produced in association with the Imperial War Museum

ISBN 0 600 586952

This title is also available in a hardback library edition
(ISBN 0 600 586944)

British Library Cataloguing-in-Publication Data
A catalogue record for this book is available from the
British Library

Printed in Hong Kong

Conceived and produced by Breslich & Foss, London
Art Director: Nigel Osborne
Design: Paul Cooper
Illustrations: Paul Ellis
Photography: Miki Slingsby

CONTENTS

THE SECOND WORLD WAR

On September 3rd 1939, Britain sent Germany an ultimatum: if Hitler did not undertake to withdraw his troops from Poland, war would be declared. Hitler refused, and first Britain, and then France, declared war on Germany. In the days that followed Canada, Australia, New Zealand and India also declared war on Germany.

People in Britain expected bombs to start falling as soon as war was declared but in fact very little happened in the first few months, and this period was known as the "Phoney War". It ended in April 1940, when German troops attacked and conquered first Norway, and then Denmark, Holland, Belgium and Luxembourg. By June German soldiers had occupied Paris, and France had surrendered. The British Expeditionary Force (B.E.F.), which had been trapped in Northern France by the German forces in May, had to be

Above: *As the likelihood of war increased, preparations were made. At Bristol zoo, the flamingo house was protected against bombs by a wall of sandbags.*

hurriedly rescued from the beaches of Dunkirk, leaving behind many tanks and guns.

Hitler then made a plan to invade Britain. But first he had to destroy the Royal Air Force (R.A.F.), so that there would be no aeroplanes to bomb the German army as it was transported

---

WAR LEADERS

Winston Churchill (1874-1965)

Churchill (*see right*) succeeded Neville Chamberlain as Prime Minister in May 1940. Churchill was a Conservative, but from 1940 to 1945 he led a coalition government, made up of politicians of all parties, working together because of the war.

Churchill knew that Britain could not win the war alone, so he appealed to President Roosevelt of America for help. Under the "Lend-Lease" system, America sold weapons to Britain on credit, because the

British goverment could not afford to pay for them.

Britain and the other countries fighting the Germans were known as "the Allies". Germany and its allies were known as "the Axis".

Adolf Hitler (1889-1945)

Germany became a dictatorship under Hitler. His Nazi party was a Fascist party, whose symbol was the swastika (*see above*). They believed in a "new order" (*see page 46*).

across the Channel. From July to September 1940, in "the Battle of Britain", British and German planes fought each other in the skies over Southern England. The *Luftwaffe*, or German Air Force, had under-estimated the number and quality of British fighter planes, and the German losses were far greater than had been expected. Hitler decided to change his plans – instead of sending the army to invade, the *Luftwaffe* would bomb Britain until it surrendered. The air raids began in September 1940, and the period of bombing which followed was known as "the Blitz", from the German word *blitzkrieg*, meaning "lightning war" *(see page 6).*

Above: *In 1941 Hitler's right hand man, Rudolf Hess, flew to Scotland to propose peace. His plane crashed and he was taken prisoner. This is part of the fusilage.*

Left: *Signposts were removed to confuse invading German soldiers. Unfortunately, it also confused the British. As the threat of invasion grew less, the signs were returned .*

Right: *A bomb-damaged London street. German cities were bombed in retaliation.*

Josef Stalin (1879-1953)
Stalin was the Soviet leader. Germany and the Soviet Union had agreed not to attack each other in 1939, but Hitler invaded the Soviet Union in 1941, and it joined the Allies.

Franklin D. Roosevelt (1882-1945)
Roosevelt was the American President. America joined the Allies in 1941, after the U.S. airbase at Pearl Harbor, Hawaii was bombed by the Japanese.

Benito Mussolini (1883-1945)
Italian Fascist leader Mussolini made an alliance with Hitler in 1939, but Italy remained neutral until 1940, when it entered the war on the German side after the invasion of France.

THE BLITZ

B y September 1939 everyone in Britain was expecting air raids. Although there had been some air raids in the First World War (1914-18), fewer than 1,500 people had been killed by bombs. The aeroplane was invented only eleven years before the First World War started, so it was not considered a very important weapon at that time. However, by 1939, aeroplanes were greatly improved and the government knew that the air raids to come would kill many more people. In the Second World War it was not only the fighting men whose lives were at risk, but, for the first time, the whole population. For this reason, it was known as a "total war".

At the start of the war, the government tried to calculate how many people would be killed by bombs, so that they could be prepared when the air raids started. They sent one million forms for recording burials to local authorities around the country, and ordered large pits to be dug for burying the dead. Thousands of coffins were ordered and piled up in readiness. They were made out of *papier mâché* or cardboard, because it was too expensive to make so many from wood. Sick people were sent home from hospitals to make room for bomb victims. Air raid precautions (A.R.P.) had begun in 1938; they included preparing air raid shelters (*see page 14*), issuing gas masks (*see page 19*) and organizing air raid wardens (*see page 36*). By the end of the war around 60,000 people had been killed – far fewer than the government had expected. The *Luftwaffe* particularly wanted to bomb factories and airfields, in order to destroy weapons or prevent them from being made. They also wanted to bomb the docks, to destroy ships containing food and weapons. However, very often the bombs would miss their intended targets and fall on houses nearby.

Beat 'FIREBOMB FRITZ'

BRITAIN SHALL NOT BURN

...D IS BRITAIN'S...

THIS IS A **REST** CENTRE

Top: *Like anti-aircraft guns and searchlights (see page 41), these barrage balloons helped to keep the German planes high in the sky so that it was harder for them to target their bombs.*

Centre: *Incendiary bomb (see page 20).*

Above: *People who were "bombed out" went to rest centres where they could wash and eat before they went off to find a new place to live. However, many homeless families stayed in these centres for weeks before they were re-housed.*

Left: *Special kits were issued for detecting mustard gas (see page 19).*

MUSTARD GAS VAPOUR

AVERAGE NUMBER OF STROKES (SPOT BLUE)	TOTAL SAFE TIME OF EXPOSURE		
	WITHOUT RESPIRATOR	WITH RESPIRATOR	
		SWEATY SKIN	COOL SKIN
5	10 MINUTES	MULTIPLY TIMES BY 2	MULTIPLY TIMES BY 4
6	20 MINUTES		
10	30 MINUTES		
25	1 HOUR		
40-50	1½ HOURS		
50-65	2 HOURS		

Air Raids

People had to follow a special procedure when an air raid was in progress. As soon as the German planes were spotted, the air raid warning siren sounded. This was known as "Moaning Minnie" because of the wailing noise it made. As soon as people heard it, they stopped what they were doing and went to an air raid shelter, where they stayed until the raiders had passed and the "all clear" was sounded. People frequently came out of the shelters to find that their homes had been destroyed by a "direct hit" and they had nothing left except the clothes they were wearing.

The Blitz began in September 1940, and for the next four and a half years there was a series of enemy raids over Britain. The first, lasting from September 1940 to May 1941, included the period known as the "London Blitz", when London was bombed every single night for over two months, as well as attacks being made on other cities. The bombings decreased until spring 1942, when there was a series of minor raids across the whole of Britain. In total, half a million homes were destroyed and four million were damaged, including Buckingham Palace. A total of 26 major British cities were bombed, although London was the primary target.

By 1944 German scientists had invented two new kinds of bombs. They were called "V" weapons. "V" stood for *Vergeltungswaffe*, meaning "Reprisal weapon". In June 1944 the first V-1 – known as the "doodlebug" – was launched. It was, literally, a flying bomb, a small pilotless plane with an explosive on board. When it ran out of fuel, it would fall to earth and explode. The V-2 was a large rocket which could carry more explosives than the V-1. There were V-2 attacks on Britain from September 1944 until the end of March 1945.

Right: *Bombed houses were often left empty. "Looting" or stealing from them was considered a serious offence, and could even be punished by hanging.*

Top: *Doctor's steel helmet.*

Centre: *Log of air raid times.*

Below: *Air raid casualty log.*

Eva Mr Allpress John Mrs Allpress Betty Nellie

THE FAMILY

WILLIAM ALLPRESS

Born in 1885, William Allpress was a railway engine driver. He was the main wage-earner in the family, and lived with his wife Alice and their children in a rented house in Clapham, London. At 55, William was too old to become a soldier, and besides, engine-driving was one of the "reserved occupations" *(see page 21)*.

ALICE ALLPRESS

Born in 1886, Alice Haynes married William Allpress when she was 18. As a housewife and mother, she had to make sure that her family got enough to eat, which was not an easy job when food was rationed *(see page 24)*. Owing to the food shortages, Alice spent a great deal of time standing in queues outside shops.

NELLIE ALLPRESS

Nellie was the eldest Allpress child still at home. Her elder sisters, Alice and Jessie, had married and left home. Born in 1911, she was 28 when war broke out. She worked in a bakery shop and did fire watching for several nights of each month *(see page 37)*.

EVA ALLPRESS

Nellie's sister Eva was born in 1913. Aged 26 when war broke out, she worked in a draper's shop, selling fabric. She joined the A.R.P. services *(see page 36)*.

Centre: *Identity cards were issued to everyone.*

Left: *Before Britain had decimal currency, money was known as "l., s. and d.". These letters stand for the Latin words* librae, solidi *and* denarii, *meaning pounds, shillings and pence. There were 12d to one shilling (now 5p) and 20 shillings – or 240d – to £1. The smallest coin was called a farthing and it was worth a quarter of one penny.*

BETTY ALLPRESS

Born in 1921, Betty was 18 when war broke out. The lampshade factory where she worked had been turned over to making seats for Lancaster bomber aircraft. In the evenings, she worked for the Women's Voluntary Service (W.V.S.), making food for the mobile canteen which was driven to bombsites to provide tea and sandwiches for rescue workers.

Below and right: *First aid kit.*

Top: *There were plenty of pieces of shrapnel lying around on bombsites. They could be fragments thrown out as the bomb exploded, or pieces of shells from anti-aircraft guns. Many children had collections of them.*

JOHN ALLPRESS

The youngest child, John, born in 1929, was only 10 when war broke out, and still at school (like his brothers and sisters, he left school when he was 14). On September 1st 1939, John and the other children from his school were evacuated to Wokingham in Berkshire (*see page 28*).

Below: R.A.F. officer's cap.

The "Call Up"

On the first day of the war, an Act of Parliament was passed introducing conscription for all men between the ages of 18 and 41. This meant that men in this age group could be called up to join the army, navy or air force and unless they were ill or doing a job which was classed as a "reserved occupation", they had to go. Some men refused to go because they thought that war was wrong, often because killing people was against their religion. They were called  "conscientious objectors", and they were usually given farming work to do instead of fighting.

Some men had already volunteered to join the armed forces in 1939 and been sent away for training. However, the conscripted men were called up very slowly, and it took almost a year to register them all. After training, many men were sent overseas to fight, and their families at home were constantly worried in case they were wounded or killed. Some soldiers, like Betty's boyfriend Cyril (*above*) were taken prisoner. Cyril was in a prisoner-of-war camp in Germany.

WILLIAM ALLPRESS

William ('Billy'), who was born in 1915, was 24 when war broke out. He was in the volunteer reserves until he was called up in 1940 to join the R.A.F. His *fiancée* was called May.

Above: *Harry's kit bag and canteen.*

HARRY ALLPRESS

Born in 1918, Harry was 21 when the war broke out. He  was called up and joined the army. He became a sergeant in the British Expeditionary Force (B.E.F.), fought in France, and was evacuated from Dunkirk. He had a girlfriend called Thelma.

69 PRIORY GROVE

 he Allpress family lived at 69, Priory Grove, Clapham, South London during the early years of the war. Their house is shown on the opposite page. There were a number of other houses in their road as well as shops, a wood yard, a school and three public houses. Betty's boyfriend Cyril lived in the next road with his mother.

 "It's a very happy house, always somebody at home, lots of people coming in and out, lots of noise. My father is the great fun of the family, and my mother works very hard looking after us all." Betty Allpress

Right: *The house was built in the nineteenth century. It is made of yellow "London Stock" bricks. During the war, the windows were criss-crossed with special tape to stop them shattering if a bomb fell nearby (see page 20). The house has no cellar. This was the safest place to spend the night during the Blitz, and those who did not have one had to make other arrangements. The Allpresses had an Anderson shelter (see below and page 14).*

The Allpresses were fortunate, because their house was not bombed during the war. However, bombs were dropped on the street: a house nearby was demolished by a direct hit and many others set alight by incendiary bombs. On the night that this happened, Mr Allpress went out into the street to see if he could help. Mrs Allpress and John took shelter in the coal cupboard under the stairs, which was the safest part of their house *(see page 12)*. They sat in there all night, while the house shook from the sound of exploding bombs and anti-aircraft guns. When the "all clear" sounded in the morning they came out, covered from head to foot in coal dust. Mr Allpress came home, completely exhausted, with white plaster from the bombed buildings all over him. When he saw his wife and son, he roared with laughter: "You look like coalmen and I look like a flour merchant!"

The Allpresses' house was not badly damaged, although some of the tiles had been blown off the roof and all the windows had cracked.

The Allpresses' Garden

The Allpresses' house did not have a bathroom, and their tin bath was kept hung up on the back wall of the house (see page 39).

The mangle was also kept outside, so that Mrs Allpress could wring out the clothes when she had washed them (see over).

The Allpresses had an Anderson shelter (see page 14) which was dug into their lawn. They planted flowers in the layer of earth on top of it.

Behind the Allpresses' garden there was a garage with a large yard where tyres were stored. The family were afraid that an incendiary bomb would fall on it and it would catch fire and choke them all with thick black smoke. Fortunately, this never happened.

INSIDE THE HOUSE

The Hall
The hall (ground floor back) like the rest of the house was lit by gas lamps. The house was heated by coal fires. Coal was kept in a cupboard under the stairs. The stirrup pump and sand bucket were kept in the hall in case an incendiary bomb fell on the house (see page 20).

The Front Room
The photograph above shows a typical wartime sitting room. There is a gramophone (record player) for entertainment. Another source of home entertainment at this time was the "wireless" or radio (see page 38). Television was still very new, with only one channel, and few people had sets. On September 1st the television shut down, and did not come back until after the war. The Allpresses' front room is at the front on the ground floor.

The Kitchen
This photograph (left) shows a typical wartime kitchen with a gas cooker. A carpet sweeper leans against the door, and a shopping bag and a gas mask container are hanging up on a hook. This house, unlike the Allpresses', has electricity. Like many people in Britain, the Allpress family did not have a telephone in their home. The Allpresses' kitchen is the large room with the table and chairs to the rear of the ground floor.

Pets

The Allpresses had a black and white cat. Thinking it was male, they called it Peter, but when it turned out to be female, they decided to keep the name anyway. Peter did not go into the shelter during air raids.The government told people to let their cats go off on their own because they are good at looking after themselves. Animals were not allowed into public shelters (*see page 15*). Dog owners took their pets into their private shelters during raids, and put cotton wool into their ears so that they would not be frightened by the noise. Some Londoners sent their pets to stay with relatives in the country.

Bedrooms

These were not used much during the war because the family slept in the Anderson shelter.

The Scullery

In the scullery (ground floor rear, behind the kitchen) there was a sink and a copper, which was a metal container for heating up water. Mrs Allpress, like most housewives, did not own a washing machine. Monday was "wash day", when she did the family's washing by hand. The copper was also used to heat water for the bath (see page 39). Food was kept in a cupboard in the scullery (most British homes did not have fridges until after the war). Instead of keeping perishable food like meat or fish in their homes, housewives went shopping every day and bought enough to last for one or two meals, so that they would be eaten before they went bad. Mrs Allpress walked to the shops to buy food because, like most families, the Allpresses did not have a car.

e Day War Broke Out

Sunday September 3rd at 11.15am, ille Chamberlain made a radio adcast to tell the British people that y were at war with Germany (*see e 4*). When he had finished, the air sirens sounded for the first time, everyone rushed to their shelters.

"The sirens went and a man rode up and down the road on a bicycle calling out "Take cover, there's an air raid on!" We ran through the garden into the shelter, pulling on our gas masks. We didn't know what was going to happen. But nothing did happen, not that day." Eva Allpress

WAKING UP

Most people who lived in London spent the night in either a private, or a public, air raid shelter. They did not always get much sleep, because the air raids and anti-aircraft guns made a lot of noise. The Allpress family had an Anderson shelter in their back garden, where they tried to get some rest at night. An Anderson shelter was a shell-like hut made of corrugated steel with two curved pieces of steel which acted as the roof and two of the walls and two flat pieces of steel which made up the other two walls, one with a door. When the shelter was put up it was six feet high, four feet wide and six and a half feet long and stood in a pit four feet deep. At least 15 inches of earth had to be heaped on top of the roof. The shelter had no floor except the earth, so it was always wet underfoot and flooded whenever it rained.

Top: *Anderson shelters saved many lives. These houses may have been totally destroyed, but the shelters are still standing.*

Above: *Anderson shelters were cramped, damp and hard to make comfortable. Some people fitted their shelters with wooden bunks, others slept on deck chairs.*

Left: *Morrison shelters, introduced in 1941, could be put up inside the house. These shelters would survive even if the house was hit, and people could be dug unharmed out of the rubble of their homes.*

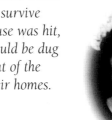

"In 1938 or 1939 the council workmen brought the shelter. You had to put it up yourself. We had the shelter for nearly a year in the back garden, but nobody bothered to dig it in. So, on September 3rd, everyone in London was digging a hole!"
Mrs Allpress

SHELTER AT HOME

The New Government
**STEEL
INDOOR 'TABLE'
SHELTER**
IS NOW AVAILABLE IN THIS DISTRICT : PARTICULARS FROM

Public Shelters and the Underground

Not everyone had an Anderson or Morrison shelter. Some people slept in the cellar and others took shelter under the stairs or went to public shelters. Trench shelters were dug in parks. They were covered with concrete or steel to give protection against bombs, but many people did not like them because they tended to fill up with filthy water. Shelters were built on the surface, too. Made from bricks or concrete, they were dark and cold with hard wooden benches and they smelt of urine. A building mistake meant that 5,000 of them were death-traps which would collapse if a bomb fell near them.

In London, some people took shelter in the Underground. Nellie and Betty travelled home from work by train and saw families laying out blankets and eating their supper on every station platform. Once, Nellie stepped off a train and nearly put her foot in a plate of salad! With thousands of people crammed together in one place and no toilets, the smell was disgusting. It was very noisy, with babies crying and children playing. Even when everyone was asleep, the noise of snoring was very loud. Some people refused to take shelter at all. They thought that if they were going to die, they might as well do so in their own beds.

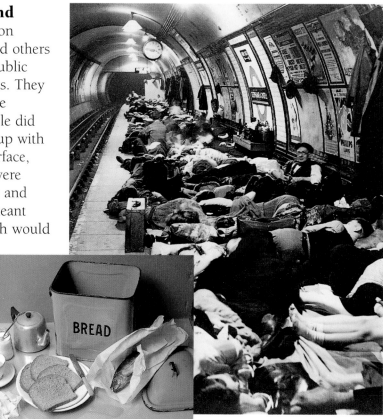

Above: *People sheltering in a tube station.*

Above left: *Breakfast foods.*

Left: *Wearing his tin hat, the postman goes on delivering letters. The number of deliveries has been reduced because many postmen have been called up to fight. Letters addressed to bombed houses are marked and returned to the sender.*

Left: *Stations were not always safe. In 1940 a bomb fell on Balham Station, severing a water main. Around 600 people were inside and 64 died when a torrent of water and rubble fell on them.*

Bottom left: *Shelter ticket.*

"You can hear the planes coming, you hear the guns firing at them, you hear them getting closer and you hear the bomb coming down and you're wondering whether it's going to come on top of the shelter..."
Nellie Allpress

15

GETTING DRESSED

Right: *The government told people to "Make Do and Mend". They suggested ways to patch and darn old clothes so that they could be worn for longer.*

The Allpress family got dressed and ready for the day. Like everyone in Britain, they had very few new clothes to wear. This was because the clothing industry was much smaller than before the war. A lot of its workers had been called up and many of the factories given over to war industries. Because of this, clothes became much more expensive. The government wanted to make sure that there were enough clothes at prices people could afford, so they introduced "Utility Clothing". Utility clothes were made from particular sorts of cloth, and cut in a special way so that the smallest possible amount was used. To save material, there were no turn-ups on men's trousers, socks could not be longer than 9½ inches (237 mm), and the number of buttons and fancy details on women's clothes was strictly limited. Trousers for women became very popular. Before the war, they were not thought to be entirely respectable, but they were more practical than skirts and many women started wearing them. Hats were hard to come by, because there was a shortage of material for making them. Instead, women wore headscarves.

Above: *There was a shortage of razor blades.*

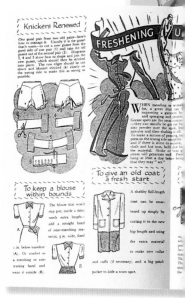

The Allpress girls tried to make their few dresses look like more by adding different coloured belts, scarves and collars to them.

Left: *Utility clothing had a special label sewn into it, like the one on this dress. Utility women's underwear like this girdle had to be made up to one of six designs. The Allpress girls bought parachute silk (see page 46) and made their own underwear.*

Clothes Rationing

Clothes were first rationed in June 1941. Rationing operated on a "points" system. Each person had a number of points in the form of coupons, and they could use them on whatever articles they wanted, provided that they could afford to pay for them. Each article was given a value of a certain number of coupons. For example, a man's shirt used up five coupons, a jacket 13, a suit 26 and a handkerchief, only one. A woman's coat used up 18 coupons, a woollen dress 11 and a pair of knickers, two. Each person got 66 coupons a year. In 1942, this was reduced to 48. Manual workers and miners were given extra coupons to buy working clothes.

Cosmetics

The government tried hard to make sure that cosmetics stayed in the shops, because they thought they helped to keep up women's spirits. However, it was quite hard to get hold of lipstick and face powder, which were the important articles – women did not use much eye make-up. It was possible to buy make-up on the "black market", but it was never very good – the face powder, for example, was usually just powdered, scented chalk.

Above: *Dressing table set.*

Above: *Clothing coupons.*
Below: *Shoes were rationed. In 1941, men's shoes "cost" seven coupons. Women's cost five, and children's three.*

Left: *Advertisements for cosmetics: stockings were in short supply so some women put brown cream on their legs to look as if they were wearing stockings. Others painted their legs with gravy powder and water – not a good idea in the summer, because it attracted flies!*

HOMES IN WARTIME

Every item that people like the Allpress family needed for their everyday life was in short supply during the war. The Allpresses soon learned to make everything last for as long as possible because when anything, even an alarm clock, broke down, it was very hard to get it repaired and almost impossible to get a new one. As the war continued, people's homes, like their clothes, became increasingly shabby. Things got broken or worn out and there was nothing in the shops to replace them.

Furniture-buying permits were only being issued to newly married people, people who were starting families and those who had been bombed out and lost everything. These permits allowed people to buy furniture up to the value of a certain number of "units". Each piece of furniture was given a price in units as well as money. Like clothes, furniture was made up to Utility designs that made use of the smallest possible amounts of wood and cloth. There were only three different designs for each article of furniture, and two qualities. The government only gave factories licences to produce furniture if they were prepared to make it to Utility standards. This also applied to items such as saucepans, pencils, umbrellas, cigarette lighters and pottery. Plates, cups and saucers were still on sale, but they were kept as simple as possible to save on materials – cups, for example, were plain white and often without handles.

Right: *A Utility armchair. Many people thought that the simple Utility designs were ugly.*

Above: *A permit for buying furniture.*

The Quota System

Owing to the shortages, each shopkeeper was given a certain amount, or quota, of unrationed goods to sell. When he had sold his quota of goods he could not order new ones, but had to wait until the next quota arrived. People grew used to seeing shops with empty shelves. The news spread fast when a shopkeeper's quota arrived and a queue formed outside his shop. People tried to be especially nice and friendly to shopkeepers so that they would keep goods such as toilet paper and razor blades on one side for them. This was known as buying something "under the counter".

Gas Masks

Each member of the Allpress family made sure that they had their gas mask before leaving the house. Most people carried their gas masks in little oblong cardboard boxes. The Allpress girls covered their boxes with fabric to make them look smart. Gas masks were issued to everyone in Britain, to take with them wherever they went. Pillar box tops were coated with special gas detecting paint, and many A.R.P. wardens were given tiny bottles of gas to sniff so that they would recognize the smell. Many people could remember the First World War, when soldiers were killed or blinded in gas attacks, and they were frightened in case gas was dropped on them by German planes. In fact, this never happened.

Above: *William married May in 1941. A traditional wedding dress with a train was out of the question because it required too much material.*

Right: *Gas warning sign and gas mask.*

Wartime Weddings

When war broke out, many couples got married quickly before the man was called up to fight. Some brides had a week's honeymoon and never saw their husbands again, because they were killed in action.

Getting married in wartime was not easy, especially if the man was serving overseas and had to wait until he had "leave" to come home. Lack of housing made it very difficult for a newly married couple to set up home. If the groom was a soldier he had to go straight back to the army, and the bride usually returned to live at her parents' house.

"It's been said that if gas is used, they'll warn us with rattles. Us girls put our hair up in curlers every night and once, when there was a raid on, my Dad came in and said 'If I were you, girls, I'd take your curlers out, because I thought I heard rattles'. You can't get your mask on if you've got curlers in. Dad was very calm about it, he didn't want to frighten us." Nellie Allpress

HOUSEWORK

Keeping the house clean and tidy in wartime was not an easy job for Mrs Allpress. Even if they landed several streets away, bombs would shake the house, bringing up dust and dirt which settled everywhere, and making plaster fall from the ceiling. Bombs also made windows shatter, and housewives often started the day by sweeping up the broken glass.

Left: *Many people were injured and killed by flying glass when windows were blown out by bombs. To try to prevent the glass exploding so violently, strips of special tape were stuck over the windows.*

Above: *People removing the remains of their belongings from their bombed house.*

The roads and pavements were covered with a thick layer of glass fragments after every raid, and as the war continued, more and more houses and shops had boarded-over windows. Plenty of water was needed after an air raid for washing and cleaning, but sometimes the supply had been cut off by the bombing.

Incendiary bombs (*see page 6*) were the most destructive weapons of the Blitz. Thousands of these were dropped on British cities, and when they struck their target, they burst into flames. The fire was easy to put out in the first few minutes, but if it was not attended to it could grow into a huge blaze which burnt for several days. The government advised people to keep fire-fighting equipment in their houses: buckets of sand, shovels and a stirrup pump for spraying water. The Allpresses went to a local park to see a demonstration of how these items were used.

Above: *Cigarette cards showing how to take air raid precautions and put out incendiary bombs.*

Below left: *Incendiary bombs had to be put out with sand. They were scooped up with these tools and put into a bucket of sand or sand was tipped over them.*

Right: *A stirrup pump was useful for putting out small fires. One person pumped up the water from a bucket, and the other sprayed it on the fire.*

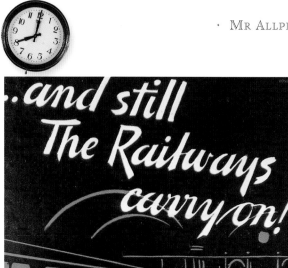

MR ALLPRESS GOES TO WORK

Mr Allpress worked as a driver of passenger trains. Train driving was one of the reserved occupations, which meant that people who did this job could not join the forces. However, many of the railway guards and porters joined up, and their jobs were taken over by women (before the war, these jobs had been done by men only).

Many of the engines and carriages were getting old and should have gone to the scrapyard, but there was nothing with which to replace them. Train and bus services were the main forms of transport. Some passenger trains were taken over by the army, and the remaining ones were always packed full of people. At every station, there were posters which said: "Is your journey really necessary?" to remind people not to travel on the trains unless their journey was important.

Above and left: Journeys were uncomfortable and trains often late because of bombs in the stations and on the lines, but the railways kept going as best they could. If anyone complained the common retort was "Don't you know there's a war on?"

Below: People like train drivers, who had to work during air raids, were issued with special anti-gas precautions like this ointment.

21

MRS ALLPRESS GOES SHOPPING

Food was in short supply in wartime, and housewives like Mrs Allpress spent hours each week queuing up to buy it. Before the war, only one-third of the food eaten in Britain had been grown in the country, and all the rest was imported in ships. During the war these ships were often sunk by German submarines. Because of this, Britain needed to produce more of its own food, so farmers ploughed up as much land as possible to

grow crops such as potatoes, wheat for bread, and fodder for cows. The likely result of the shortages was that food prices would go up, and poorer people were worried in case the better-off bought all the food and left nothing for them. When the government introduced the system of sharing out food, known as "rationing", people liked the idea because it was fair. The government stopped food prices rising and made all the shops charge the same.

Above: This figure, known as "Chad" was often drawn by wartime graffiti artists. He was always complaining: "Wot, no – ?" It might be cigarettes, sweets, beer or anything that was in short

Rationing

When war broke out, a national register was set up, and everyone was given an identity card (*see page 8*). By January 1940 ration books had been issued, and butter, sugar, ham and bacon were all "on the ration". Meat was rationed in March 1940, and then tea, margarine, lard and cheese in July. Jam was rationed in March 1941, followed by eggs in June and milk in November. Sweets were rationed in July 1942.

In December 1941 a "points" system was introduced for unrationed food such as spam and biscuits. It worked in the same way as the clothing coupons (*see page 17*); everyone had 16 points to "spend" per month, and the different foods were given points "prices" according to how difficult they were to obtain.

Large families, like the Allpresses, were better off than single people, because they could pool their rations.

Above: A food queue.
Right: Even the Royal Family had ration books.

Left: Ration books and a special handbag with a compartment for holding a gas mask.

Left: *Rationed food for one person. This amount of food, which varied by a few ounces, had to last for a whole week. Vegetables did not have to be rationed because there were plenty of them. Bread was not rationed until 1946, after the war had ended.*

Average Weekly Rations for One Person During Wartime
2 pts milk
4oz (100g) bacon
1s. 2d worth of beef, pork, veal or mutton – just under 1lb (550g)
4oz (100g) butter
2oz (50g) cheese
4oz (100g) margarine
2oz (50g) lard
8oz sugar (225g)
8oz (225g) jam
2oz (50g) tea
1 egg
3oz (75g) sweets

"We all took sugar in our tea, and Mum didn't want to waste it on that. So she shovelled it into our tea until it was so sweet we got fed up and stopped taking it!"
Eva Allpress

The Allpress family's ration books were registered with local shops, and Mrs Allpress had to go to the same butcher, grocer and dairy every week to buy the rationed foods. Every shopkeeper had a number of registered customers. He only received enough rationed goods for these customers, and could not sell them to anyone else.

As the war continued and the shortages grew worse, British people were introduced to many new sorts of food. When it became impossible to get white flour, Nellie's shop and the other bakeries sold a "National Loaf" of greyish-brown bread. Many people had never eaten brown bread, and complained that it tasted disgusting and made them ill. Dried eggs were also introduced; one packet (equal to 12 ordinary eggs) for each person every month. These were useful for making cakes and could be eaten scrambled, although some people did not like the taste. By 1945 horsemeat and whalemeat had started appearing in butchers' shops. There were few treats available during the war: chocolate was very scarce, and oranges and bananas disappeared completely. People joked that they had forgotten what an orange looked like, and many younger children had never actually seen one.

Above: *A wartime larder. Some tinned food, such as the dried milk and eggs shown here, was imported from America under the "Lend-lease" agreement (see page 4). Cod liver oil, containing Vitamins A and D, was given free to all children under five by the Ministry of Food.*

EATING IN WARTIME

T he government created a new ministry to deal with food rationing and to control food production. It was called the Ministry of Food, and Lord Woolton was given the job of Minister of Food. The Ministry wanted to make sure that people would eat properly and stay healthy. They gave information on healthy eating in a daily radio programme called "Kitchen Front", and "food facts" were given in magazines. They also published books and leaflets with recipes for making the most of the food ration. The "radio doctor", Charles Hill, gave a talk each day explaining why particular types of food were good to eat and how they should be cooked. He was always telling people to eat potatoes and carrots, because there were always plenty of these vegetables. The government put up posters with pictures of characters called "Potato Pete" and "Dr Carrot" (*see below*) to encourage people to eat them in specially made-up recipes such as carrot jam, curried carrots, potato cutlets and "Mock Goose", which was really a mixture of potatoes, apples and cheese (many "Mock" recipes were issued by the Ministry, including Mock Cream and Mock Duck). People were also encouraged to experiment with foods they had not used before such as nettles, dandelion leaves and dock leaves.

"*You get bored with having the same thing, but you never go hungry. Fresh eggs are what I miss most. Powdered eggs don't taste the same, but they go a lot further.*" Betty Allpress

Restaurants

People who ate in restaurants did not have to hand over any food coupons when they paid for their meal. However, because the government was worried about fairness, restaurant meals were limited to a main course only, and no more than five shillings could be charged. This rule did not apply to the smarter restaurants, however, and they charged a lot of money for their better-quality meals.

There were also "British restaurants" which were run by local authorities. They were self-service, and sold cheap and unrationed meals. These were useful for workers who wanted a hot meal but could not afford to eat in a restaurant. Eating out also helped people to make their rations last for the whole week.

Left: *Ministry of Food posters. Some people started keeping hens in their back gardens. They were given chicken food instead of their weekly egg. "Pig clubs" were also popular – the members bought a pig and fattened it up on kitchen scraps.*

"Along the roads there are little tubs for you to put food in – your peelings and scrapings that they are collecting for the pigs. We always do that."
Nellie Allpress

Above: *Housewives putting their scraps into a "pig bin".*
Left and right: *A wartime meal: Lord Woolton pie, cabbage and a Norfolk pudding, made with rice and dried fruit.*

Lord Woolton Pie

This recipe was invented by the Chef at the Savoy Hotel. This version of it was issued by the Ministry of Food. These quantities serve five to six people.

Take 1lb each of diced potatoes, cauliflower, swedes and carrots, three or four spring onions, if possible one teaspoonful of vegetable extract and one tablespoonful of oatmeal. Cook altogether for 10 mins, with just enough water to cover. Stir occasionally to prevent the mixture from sticking. Allow to cool; put into a pie dish, sprinkle with chopped parsley, and cover with a crust of potatoes or wholemeal pastry. Bake in a moderate oven until the pastry is nicely brown and serve hot with a brown gravy.

JOHN IS EVACUATED

A few days before war broke out, John Allpress, along with over 800,000 other schoolchildren, was moved into the country. This was called "being evacuated". Parents knew that the cities were far more likely to be bombed than the countryside, and they wanted their children to be as safe as possible. The children went to stay with foster parents. People called "Billeting Officers" had the job of seeing that all the children had somewhere to stay. The night that John was evacuated, Mrs Allpress was very worried because she had no idea where he was or if he had arrived safely.

All the children in each school were evacuated together, with their teachers, so that the school could be set up again in the country. Pregnant women were also evacuated, and babies and very young children were evacuated along with their mothers. Although these were the only people evacuated by the government, many people went to stay with relatives who lived in the country and some went to live in country hotels.

Above: *Children, pregnant women and invalids were given extra milk rations – usually one pint a day. Free milk was provided for the poorest mothers and children.*

"When I was evacuated, there were red London double-decker buses, masses of them, taking the whole school, teachers and pupils, down to Wokingham. That's about forty miles from London, but it felt like the end of the Earth. I felt very unhappy, it was my first time away from home."
John Allpress

Top: *Toddlers were given red and blue gas masks, called "Mickey Mouse" gas masks to make them seem more fun to wear.*

Above left: *These "gas helmets" were issued to babies. The helmet was sealed around the baby's head and air pumped in through the tube.*

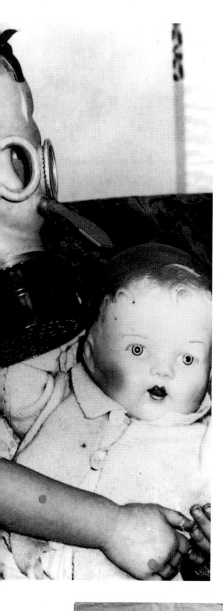

The Journey

The evacuees travelled by bus or train (see page 21). Like many children, John arrived feeling very tired and anxious about what was going to happen next. He and his schoolmates – it was a boys' school – went into a local hall and were given a drink of milk. Then the people who had promised to be foster parents arrived. They looked at the boys and picked out the ones they liked. Most of the evacuees looked dirty and upset after their long journey, and the people did not always want to take them into their homes. Big boys were often chosen by farmers because they would be strong enough to help on the farm. If the evacuees were girls, the older ones were usually picked first because they could help with the housework. Many people, like the lady who took John, arrived saying they would only take one evacuee, but the billeting officer persuaded them to take two. Others took an extra child because their chosen evacuee had a brother or sister and refused to leave them. All the foster parents were given a small sum of money each week in return for looking after an evacuee.

Above left: *This school satchel has a large pocket on the front for carrying a gas mask.*

Below left: *Toy-making materials were needed for making weapons, and paper toys like this were amongst the few left on sale. There was not much for Mr and Mrs Allpress to buy John for his birthday or for Christmas, although the government did allow some toys to be made for Christmas in 1942 and 1943, to make it more cheerful. Plane spotting was a popular game. Many booklets about planes like the one shown and guides for recognizing aircraft were published.*

29

LIFE IN THE COUNTRY

A local church hall was the new home of John's school. Other schools were re-housed in country mansions, or were simply merged with village schools. All the young male teachers had been called up, and the elderly teachers who came out of retirement to take their places were not always good at keeping order.

City children found life in the country very strange and there were many stories about children who did not know that apples grew on trees or that milk came from cows. Evacuees from poor families often did not have enough clothes, some were very dirty, and some had headlice, which upset the foster parents very much. Many children wet their beds because they were frightened at being in a strange place, and got into trouble with their foster parents, who thought they had dirty habits. But many evacuees, like John, were simply homesick. John missed his parents and sisters and felt very unhappy.

John's parents and sisters often visited him, and, when they realized that he was not going to settle down happily in his new surroundings, they decided to bring him home. They were not the only parents to make this decision – during the "Phoney War" period, three-quarters of all evacuees returned to their homes. A lot of parents, like the Allpresses, could not bear to see their children so miserable, and thought "if we're going to die, let's all die together".

As the evacuees returned to their families, the city schools, many of which had been made into rest centres (*see page 6*) had to be re-opened. Like many children, John fell behind at school because of these interruptions, and found it hard to catch up again.

"*We got off the bus and went into a big hall. People were coming and taking boys and I didn't know where they went to... there were two of us left at the end, and the lady had to be pressed to take one extra. I don't think she really wanted either of us. On the Sunday it was on the radio that we were at war with Germany, and I thought, well, now I'm going to be stuck here forever.*"
John Allpress

Above right: *All the children were labelled, so that they would not get lost on the journey.*

Above and far right: *Mrs Allpress was given a list of things to pack for John.*

Government Evacuation Scheme

Clothing required:
Overcoat or mackintosh

Girls: 1 vest, 1 pair of knickers, 1 petticoat, 2 pairs of stockings, handkerchiefs, 1 slip, 1 blouse, 1 cardigan.

Boys: 1 vest, 1 pair of knickers, 1 pair of trousers, 2 pairs of socks, handkerchiefs, 1 pullover or jersey.

Night wear: comb, towel soap, face-cloth, tooth-brush, boots or shoes, plimsolls.

Food: Sandwiches, packets of nuts and seedless raisins, dry biscuits, barley sugar (rather than chocolate), apple, orange.

All should have gas masks.

"I was there for about six months. Mum and Dad saw that I was so homesick, and they said, "Well, enough's enough". I was so happy when they came to fetch me. A lot of the boys at my school were homesick. Most of them have come back home." John Allpress

Right: *Government posters told mothers not to bring their children back to the cities, but this was hard for women like Mrs Allpress who knew that their children were unhappy living with foster parents.*

SALVAGE AND SAVINGS

Material for making weapons was urgently needed, and the government encouraged "Salvage Drives" when people collected scrap metal, bones (used for making glue), bottles and rags. Paper had to be recycled, because very little new paper was being made. Posters, and even bus tickets, encouraged people to save paper, and some people even gave books to be recycled.

Children like John Allpress spent hours looking for scrap to take to the collecting yard, which was piled high with everything from old farmyard machinery, bicycles and prams to coat hangers and kettles.

Workmen came to take down the iron railings outside the Allpresses' house, leaving behind the concrete base where the railings had stood with a row of holes in it (see below). Soon, the railings had been removed from most of the houses and parks in London.

There were also "savings drives" when people were encouraged to lend money to the government by buying savings stamps. Each savings drive was for one particular aspect of the war: there was a "Warships Week" and a "Wings for Victory Week". There were also "Spitfire Funds". People from a particular town clubbed together to raise enough money to build one fighter plane. The plane, usually a Spitfire, would have the town's name painted on it. A price list showed people how their money was spent: for example, a person who gave sixpence paid for one rivet, and someone who gave £22 paid for a small bomb.

Above left: *The "Squanderbug" on this poster warned people not to buy things they did not really need, so that material needed for weapons was not used up on other things.*

Below left: *This book was produced to remind people how important it was to collect scrap.*

Above and right: *Lord Beaverbrook, the Minister of Aircraft Production, appealed to people to give up their aluminium saucepans to be turned into fighter planes. Mrs Allpress could not spare any of her pots and pans, but many people, including the Royal Family, gave saucepans, and thousands were collected. Unfortunately, they did not contain enough high-grade aluminium to be of any use in making aircraft.*

DIG FOR VICTORY

T he government wanted people to grow their own vegetables, so that there was less need for imported food. They put up posters urging people to "dig for victory". The Allpress family grew mustard-and-cress on a piece of flannel in a saucer, and had it in sandwiches as their Sunday treat. Betty started growing carrots. Runner beans were grown in the garden, and in 1943, Mr Allpress got a little plot of land – called an "allotment" – beside the railway track, where he grew many different sorts of vegetables.

Everywhere, gardens and public parks, including Hyde Park, were dug up and turned into vegetable patches. Some people even grew their vegetables beside football pitches.

Above: *Some people turned the tops of their Anderson shelters into vegetable patches.*

Right: *The "Dig for Victory" campaign was very successful. The government printed and distributed over ten million leaflets telling people how to grow vegetables.*

LETTERS HOME

L ike millions of others who had sons, brothers or husbands serving overseas, the Allpresses wrote regularly to Harry and William (*see page 9*) and waited anxiously for their letters. Betty wrote to her boyfriend Cyril, who was a prisoner of war (P.O.W.). People did not want to add to the problems of their loved ones by worrying them, so they often wrote letters which made things sound better than they really were. Those in London might write that no bombs had fallen near them when the next street had been demolished, or a soldier might write that he was "keeping his spirits up" when in fact he was frightened and miserable. S.W.A.L.K. ("Sealed with a loving kiss") was often written on the back of the envelope.

"When Harry came back from France through Dunkirk we didn't hear anything for weeks. Then the postman brought us a little thing like a luggage label, just to say he'd arrived in England and he'd be writing soon. It was a great relief to us."
Nellie Allpress

Above right: *Letters written by men in the forces and P.O.W.s had to be censored before they were sent, to make sure that they did not contain any information which would help the enemy if the letter got into their hands. "First captive" cards (top right) were sent by soldiers when they arrived at P.O.W. camps so that their families would know what had happened to them. The Allpresses received the postcard (bottom right) when Harry returned from Dunkirk.*

Left: *A newspaper with headline about the D-Day invasion in June 1944. Newspapers were censored by the Ministry of Information because they were read by the Germans, and it was important not to give away military secrets. By the time of D-Day, British people were confident of winning the war. However victory had not been at all certain in the previous years, and for this reason journalists were asked to be careful how they reported things, so that they did not upset people and make them feel that the war was being lost.*

Food Parcels

Although both Germany and Britain had agreed to follow rules about the treatment of prisoners, men in P.O.W. camps did not get enough food to keep them healthy. The Red Cross Organization aimed to send one food parcel a week to every British P.O.W., although the situation in Europe meant that these often arrived late or not at all. The parcels included condensed milk, cheese, tinned meat and other sorts of food.

There were also "next of kin" parcels. Cyril's mother was allowed to send him one parcel every three months. The parcel could not weigh more than 10lb, and it could only contain certain items – for example, chocolate was the only food allowed. Cyril's mother had to send her parcel to the Red Cross "Packing Centre" so that it could be checked before being sent. Relatives' parcels usually contained clothes and soap, although the Red Cross also sent clothing parcels. Those prisoners who had no families were usually "adopted" by someone who would send them a parcel.

Besides food and clothes, the Red Cross also sent each man a weekly ration of either 50 cigarettes or 2oz of tobacco. Relatives could send more if they liked, and they could also send books.

"I save up my ration of chocolate to send to Cyril at the P.O.W. camp. When I grow carrots, I take them with me to work to eat instead." Betty Allpress

Right: *A Red Cross parcel.*

Below: *People knitted socks to send to the soldiers.*

Superstition

People tended to be more superstitious during the war, because of the danger. Some people thought that the same building could not be bombed twice, and others looked at the tea leaves at the bottom of their cup to see if they could "read" the future in them.

One month Cyril's regular letter did not arrive, and Betty, who was not superstitious, let a girl at her work read her tea leaves. The girl said that when Betty got home, there would be a letter from Cyril, but not in his writing, because he had hurt his hand. That night, Betty found a letter at home from Cyril's P.O.W. camp, but she did not recognize the writing. The letter said that Cyril and another man had crawled through the camp fence to get some potatoes from a field because they were hungry. They were caught as they crawled back with their potatoes, and one of the guards had trodden on Cyril's hand and injured it.

Mum gets very worried. She'll be on the doorstep an hour before the postman comes, waiting to hear if the boys are all right. We always say to her, "If it's bad news, you would hear." But we are all worried about them..." Eva Allpress

CIVILIAN SERVICES

Many people became part of the "civil defence" force during the war. Some took full-time jobs, others, like Nellie, Betty and Eva, worked part-time, and others simply helped out whenever they could. There were many different jobs to be done. If a bomb had fallen, several streets of houses might be reduced to rubble. The local air raid warden, who knew where everyone lived, would report the "incident" from his post. This was a small building, surrounded by sand-bags, which contained a telephone and a map of the area. The firemen came to put out any fires and an ambulance arrived, along with a "mobile first aid post" (a car) with nurses and a doctor. Wounded people were carried out of the wreckage and treated. If they were trapped, the heavy rescue service would dig them out. Those that could be seen were given tea, and morphine if they were in pain. Rescue workers often had to burrow deep into the rubble to find people who were pinned underneath bricks and planks. Dead bodies were labelled (*see above left*) so that they could be identified.

Home Guard

The first appeal for men to join the Home Guard (then known as the Local Defence Volunteers) was in May 1940 when Britain was in danger of invasion. Men between the ages of 17 and 65 were asked to volunteer. At first, they did not have any weapons. People gave them guns and they devised some home-made weapons (*see below*). Some even armed themselves with pitchforks and golf clubs! However, they were gradually issued with regulation weapons and uniforms, and by 1942 they were being given proper training.

Home Guard duties included guarding the coastline and defending aerodromes and factories. They also served on anti-aircraft gun sites.

Right: *A.R.P. uniform.*

Far right: *The W.V.S. ran a service for people who needed to find out if their friends and relatives were safe after an air raid.*

Women's Voluntary Service

The Women's Voluntary Service (W.V.S.) did many jobs during the war, from selling war savings stamps door to door (*see page 32*) to running rest centres (*see page 6*). They also ran clothing centres to supply fresh clothes to people who had been bombed out and lost everything except what they were wearing, which was usually torn by glass splinters and covered with dust. They also ran mobile canteens which travelled to bombed sites. For two nights each week, Betty worked for the W.V.S. in the town hall preparing sandwiches for them.

Far left: *A.R.P. first aid kit.*
Left: *An A.R.P. warden carries a child from a bombed house.*

Auxiliary Fire Service

During the Blitz, incendiary bombs (*see page 20*) started so many fires that there were not enough firemen to extinguish them, and the Auxiliary Fire Service (A.F.S.) was formed to help. A.F.S. men and women worked for 48-hour shifts, fighting fires, and some collapsed from exhaustion. People were asked to "fire watch" in order to prevent some of the fires.

Above: *A.R.P. helmet ("W" stands for warden) and a hook for pulling down damaged ceilings in bombed houses.*

"I'd like to go out on the mobile canteen itself but I'm too tall – they'd have to cut a hole in the roof to carry me! But we've all got to have two jobs, whatever it is. You do get tired, but you don't take any notice of it." Betty Allpress

Fire Watching

Men who worked for less than 60 hours per week and did not have Home Guard or other Civil Defence duties were required to do 48 hours fire watching every month, as were women who worked for less than 55 hours per week. Nellie Allpress did fire watching at the bakery where she worked. When she was on duty she had to spend the night at the shop (a camp bed was provided). If there was an air raid, she and another worker had to patrol the bakery and the shops nearby and look out for fires. They also had to use the stirrup pump and other equipment to put out any small fires.

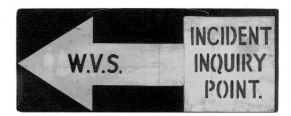

Entertainment

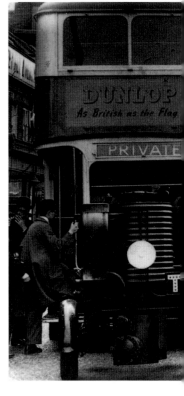

Entertainment was limited during the war. Transport was often a problem – petrol was rationed (*see opposite*), bus queues were long and buses often had to go on long detours to avoid unexploded bombs. During the worst of the Blitz, most theatres shut, re-opening as the bombing grew less. Many people went to the cinema, and *Gone with the Wind* was one of the most popular films. It was hard for the Allpress girls to get to the cinema, but on Saturdays they went to dances at the A.R.P. centre. It was near their house, so they could walk home afterwards.

Entertaining at home was also limited, because food was rationed. Going to somebody's house for dinner meant taking your own butter, and, usually, staying for the night. Pubs were still popular. Beer was not rationed, but it was watered down, and each pub had a beer "quota" (*see page 18*) Cigarettes were not rationed, but as most adults smoked, they were often hard to get.

Above left: *People were asked to switch the radio off when they weren't listening, to save power*

> *We don't go to the cinema much, because it's hard to get home afterwards. We went into London to see a film, and the siren went while we were there, but we didn't take any notice, and when we came out there were fire engines everywhere. We couldn't get home quick enough!"* Nellie Allpress

Below: *These posters warned people not to reveal any information that might help the enemy.*

Radio

Most homes in Britain had a radio. Besides news and information, there were music programmes, talks, and comedy shows. The Allpresses enjoyed listening to dance music and sometimes listened to the comedy programmes *Bandwagon* and *ITMA*. *ITMA* stood for "It's that man again" and starred a popular comedian called Tommy Handley. The famous singer Vera Lynn had her own programme.

A British man called William Joyce, who was a supporter of Hitler, made broadcasts to Britain from Germany. Known as "Lord Haw Haw" because of his posh voice, he talked about what was happening in the war and tried to convince the British people that they were losing the war. Some people were frightened by his broadcasts, but many made fun of his accent.

Reading was also popular, although the paper shortage meant that few new books were printed. When the sirens sounded in the evening, Nellie, Eva and Betty often took a candle and a book into the Anderson shelter and read aloud to each other.

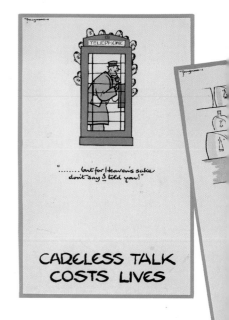

"........ but for Heaven's sake don't say I told you!"

CARELESS TALK COSTS LIVES

Left: *At the start of the war, gas companies tried to get people to fuel their cars with gas. However, a gas bag like this one only held 5.72 cubic metres of gas – which fuelled the car for as long as one gallon of petrol. Gas bags were not popular, and were rarely seen after 1942.*

Below: *Petrol coupons*

Petrol Rationing

This was introduced three weeks after the war started. Petrol was imported from overseas, and during the war, seamen on petrol tankers ran enormous risks bringing it to Britain. A lot of this fuel was needed by the forces, so there was not much left over for private cars. At first, all car owners were given a small ration, but this was stopped in 1942, and people had to prove that driving was essential to their work or their health in order to get petrol coupons.

Right: *Football matches continued, although many of the stars, such as Stanley Matthews, had joined the forces. Many people stopped attending matches because they were afraid of being caught in a large crowd if a bomb dropped.*

BATHTIME

Most people used coal to heat their homes. In 1942 there was a coal shortage because the war industries needed extra fuel, and many younger miners had joined the forces. The government did not want to ration fuel, so they appealed to people to save it by using only five inches of bathwater. People painted a black line round the bath (*see above*) so that they would not overfill it.

The Allpresses washed every day, but, like many families, they only bathed once a week. On bath night, they took the tin bath from the back wall of the house (*see page 10*) and brought it into the scullery where it was filled with hot water. Dirty water was emptied down the drain in the garden.

Below: *In February 1942, soap was rationed to 16oz per month. This is one month's soap ration.*

THE BLACKOUT

Every evening, half an hour after the sun had set, Mrs Allpress went round the house "doing the blackout". It took her five or ten minutes to make quite sure that there was no light to be seen from any window of the house. If she left one single chink of light, a policeman or an air raid warden would knock on the door to tell her. Mrs Allpress was allowed to open her curtains half an hour before sunrise, when the blackout was lifted. The purpose of the blackout was to make it as difficult as possible for German bomber pilots to locate towns and factories, so that they would not know exactly where they were dropping their bombs.

The blackout started on September 1st 1939, two days before the outbreak of war. Mrs Allpress went to the shops and bought thick, black material to use as curtains. Everywhere, people were buying blinds, curtains, blackout paint, cardboard, brown paper, drawing pins and anything else they could use to make sure that no light could be seen from their houses. All the houses, offices and factories in Britain had to have their "blackout" in place. Factories with windows too large to be curtained or covered by shutters had to paint them over with black paint, and use artificial light all the time.

wear somethi

LOOK OUT IN THE BLACK

"When Billy was on leave, he came home one night in the blackout and walked straight into a lamp post. People thought he was drunk, but he wasn't, and he'd cut his face." Mrs Allpress

Above left: *People could buy luminous armbands and buttons to make themselves more visible. Cycling in the blackout was extremely dangerous. These black disks could be used to mask the bicycle lamps.*

Left: *Different types of lamp covers.*
Centre left: *Drivers had to fit these special hoods on to their headlights, so that only a thin strip of light could be seen.*

Far left: *Luminous umbrella cover.*

"Everyone uses the same type of torch. They take No 8 batteries and of course everyone wants those so you have to spend hours searching for them in the shops. If you're a regular customer they'll sell you one, otherwise it's "Sorry, sold out!" Betty Allpress

Issued by THE NATIONAL "SAFETY FIRST" ASSOCIATION (Inc.), Terminal House, 52, Grosvenor Gardens, London, S.W. 1
BCL/11

Going to Bed

In the evening the Allpress family settled down to try to get some sleep in the Anderson shelter. At the beginning of the war, there were only deckchairs to sleep on, but later two bunks were added, making it a little more comfortable. They slept fully clothed, with the girls wearing trousers and warm jumpers. A suitcase full of clothes and underwear was kept in the shed at the bottom of the garden, in case the house was hit and everything lost. If anyone wanted to go to the toilet in the night, they had to go into the house. They grabbed a torch and ran across the garden and back as fast as they could.

Left: *One of a number of posters telling people to be careful in the blackout.*

Below: *Searchlights were shone upwards into the sky so that German bombers could be located and targetted by the anti-aircraft guns.*

Left: *Some farmers painted white stripes on their cows so that drivers would be able to see them in the blackout.*

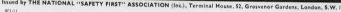

In the first weeks of the war the blackout was total. All the street lights were turned off and cars could not use their headlights. People were forbidden to use torches to get about, and fined if they even lit a match in the street. As a result, there were twice as many road accidents as before. Many people injured themselves by walking into trees, and although white stripes had been painted on kerbs, people often tripped over them.

By October the government had changed the rules to allow people to carry small torches, provided they were dimmed with tissue paper and shone downwards. Drivers were permitted to use their headlights if they were masked (*see opposite*), and this reduced the number of accidents. Passengers on trains and buses had to sit in near-darkness, and bus conductors could barely see to give people tickets. The blackout ended in September 1944, when it became a "dimout". However, many street lamps had been destroyed in the Blitz, and it took a long time to repair them.

VE DAY

V E stands for Victory in Europe. The beginning of the end of the war in Europe was the D-Day invasion on June 6th 1944, when British and American troops successfully invaded German-held France. In August the German commandant in Paris surrendered. In spring 1945 British and American troops began to advance on Germany from France. The Russian troops moved towards it through Austria, and in early April they captured the Austrian capital, Vienna. When they heard the reports of these victories, people in Britain knew that it was only a matter of time before the war was won. On April 25th the Russian army surrounded Berlin, where Hitler had his underground bunker. Hitler committed suicide on April 30th, and on May 7th Germany surrendered.

In Britain, it was announced that the following day, May 8th, would be "VE day", a national holiday to celebrate victory. Everywhere, people hung out banners and Union Jacks. They sang, danced, cheered, let off fireworks and built bonfires to burn guys that were dressed up to look like Hitler. Churchill broadcast a special message on the radio, and large crowds gathered to cheer him outside the House of Commons. He made several public appearances, waving to the crowd and giving his "V for Victory" sign (see right). When night fell, all the lights, including the searchlights, were turned on, so that the cities looked as bright as possible.

Far left: *Victory banner.*
Left: *Civil defence workers got certificates to say that they had served in the war. Harry received this certificate* (below). *He was also awarded the Military Medal.*

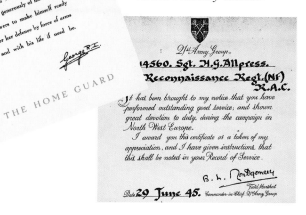

Demobbing

The word "demob" is short for demobilize, meaning to take out of military service. At the end of the war, thousands of men and women in the armed forces had to be demobbed. The first to leave the army were engineers and builders, who were needed to help rebuild houses. The remainder were demobbed in order of their age and length of service (older men, and those who had served longest, were demobbed first).

"People are rushing out into the streets, hugging each other and dancing around, you can make as much noise as you like and not worry about it. I can't believe it, the war is finished, I just cannot believe it!" Betty Allpress

Each man received eight weeks' pay, and free clothes, which included a "demob suit" (*see right*) and a hat. William, Harry and Cyril received these when they were demobbed in 1946. Women were given money and clothing coupons to spend on whatever clothes they liked. Some soldiers found it hard to adjust to ordinary life. A "Resettlement Advice Service" was set up to help them.

After the War

In many families, sons, brothers, fathers and husbands would not be coming back, because they had been killed in action, and many men in the forces had no family to come back to, because their relatives had been killed in the Blitz and their homes destroyed. The Allpress family knew that they were very lucky to be alive and uninjured, and to have William, Harry and Cyril coming home to them. Harry and his girlfriend Thelma were married in 1945, and Betty and Cyril in 1946. Clothes were still rationed, so Betty hired a wedding dress from the costume department of a film studio. Thelma wore an evening dress which she trimmed with a piece of net curtain to make it look more like a wedding gown!

HOME FRONT TIME CHART

of human conflict was so much owed by so many to so few".

A "front" means a line of battle where two opposing armies meet to attack each other, and the term "home front" was used in the war to mean the war work and civilian defence activities in Britain. George VI (reigned 1936-1952) was king during the war, with his queen, Elizabeth (now the Queen Mother).

1938

Gas masks issued to the public. Distribution of Anderson shelters.

September Neville Chamberlain and Hitler meet at Munich. Chamberlain returns saying there will be "peace in our time".

1939

March Air raid precautions service set up.

April Conscription begins.

August 11th Trial run for the blackout.

September 1st German troops march into Poland. Blackout begins.

September 1st-3rd Mass evacuation of schoolchildren, including John Allpress, pregnant women, and children under five with their mothers.

September 3rd At 9am the British ultimatum that German troops be withdrawn from Poland is handed over to the German government. It is not answered, and expires at 11am. Britain and France declare war on Germany. Men aged between 18 and 41 are made liable for conscription into the army, navy or air force. The beginning of the "Phoney War" period.

September 29th National Register set up. Identity cards issued.

October Barrage balloons go up. Harry Allpress called up. Petrol rationed.

1940

January Food rationing begins. Bacon, ham, sugar and butter rationed. Cyril called up and joins the Royal Army Medical Corps.

March Meat rationed. William Allpress called up.

April Lord Woolton appointed Minister of Food. The "Phoney War" ends.

May 10th Churchill succeeds Chamberlain as Prime Minister, presiding over a coalition government.

May 14th First appeal for men to join the Local Defence Volunteers (known as the Home Guard after July 1940). People cover any piece of countryside on which an invading plane could land with obstacles, such as old cars. Pill boxes (small concrete huts for housing machine guns) and tank traps (lines of large concrete "teeth") are erected in the countryside.

May 22nd Emergency Powers (Defence) Act passed to allow the government to make new defence rules without the consent of Parliament.

June 5th Harry Allpress evacuated from Dunkirk beach, along with other members of the British Expeditionary Force. Britain in danger of invasion by the German army. Churchill gives his "we shall fight on the beaches" speech in the House of Commons.

June 10th Italy declares war on Britain and France.

July Tea, margarine, lard and cheese rationed.

July-September The Battle of Britain – air battle between the R.A.F. and the Luftwaffe over Britain. Churchill praises the R.A.F. for "winning" the battle. "Never in the field

September 7th The beginning of the Blitz. London is raided for 76 consecutive nights (except November 2nd). The East End is badly bombed because it is near the docks. As well as London, major cities such as Southampton and Liverpool are bombed.

September 11th Anti-aircraft guns brought to London.

September 13th Buckingham Palace hit by a bomb. The Queen says "I'm glad we've been bombed. It makes me feel I can look the East End in the face".

October Neville Chamberlain dies.

November 14th Coventry severely bombed. The whole of the city centre is burnt out, with loss of water, drainage, public transport and telephones. Coventry cathedral is destroyed.

December 29th Second 'Fire of London'. The city is ablaze but St. Paul's Cathedral is saved. It becomes a symbol of the survival of London and Britain.

1941

May 10th The last night of the London Blitz. Westminster Abbey and the Tower of London are hit, and the House of Commons is burnt down. It takes eleven days to extinguish all the fires.

March Jam, marmalade, treacle and syrup rationed.

May The Allpresses leave the house at Priory Grove and move to another part of London.

June Eggs rationed. Clothes rationed – each person receives 66 coupons per year. Germany invades Russia. Cyril is taken prisoner by the Germans in Crete. He is taken to Stalag VIIIB P.O.W. camp in Germany.
July Male conscription extended to those aged 51.
September Firewatching made compulsory. Morrison shelters introduced.
November Milk rationed.
December Introduction of points scheme for food. Japanese attack Pearl Harbor, Hawaii. U.S.A. joins the Allies. Women aged between 20 and 30 made liable to conscription. William and May are married.

1942

January First American soldiers (called G.I.s after the words "Government Issue" on their equipment) land in Britain.
February Soap rationed.
March Petrol ends for private cars.
April-June The "Baedeker" raids. These were a series of German air raids directed at provincial towns and cities, all of which were known for their beautiful buildings. The chosen targets included Bath, York and Canterbury. "Baedeker" was the name of a well-known series of guide books for tourists. Clothing coupons cut to 48 per year.
July Sweets rationed.
November 1st The government prohibits manufacturers to make any furniture except Utility styles, in order to save raw materials.
November-December Members of the Allied forces, including William Allpress, land in North Africa, in "Operation Torch".

1943

"Tip and run" raids on towns and cities in Britain continue throughout the year.

May John Allpress leaves school and goes to work at a factory for aircraft parts.
July Conscription for women extended to those aged 51.

1944

January-April Series of heavy air raids on London and other major cities, known as the "Little Blitz".
May-June Allied forces mass in Southern England for D-day invasion.
June 6th D-day – Allied forces land on the coast of France for the invasion of German-occupied Europe. Harry Allpress returns to France on D+11.

June 12th First V-1 bomb falls on Britain. The heaviest V-1 raids occur between June and August, but they continue until March 1945.
September 8th First V-2 rocket falls on Britain. V-2 bombing raids continue until March 1945.
September 11th Compulsory Home Guard parades end.
September 17th Blackout ends. William Allpress goes to Italy.

1945

April 12th American President Roosevelt dies. Harry S. Truman becomes President.
April 25th Allied forces surround Berlin.
April 29th German forces in Italy surrender.
April 30th Hitler commits suicide.
May 8th VE (Victory in Europe) Day.
May 15th Harry returns to England.
May 16th Harry and Thelma are married.

June Cyril is released from P.O.W. camp and returns home.
July General election – Labour gains power. Clement Attlee becomes Prime Minister.
August 6th American forces drop atomic bomb on Hiroshima, Japan.
August 9th American forces drop atomic bomb on Nagasaki, Japan.
August 14th Japan surrenders.
August 15th VJ Day (VJ stands for Victory in Japan).
November Trial of 24 Nazi war criminals at Nuremberg, lasting until October 1946.
December William Allpress returns to England.

1946

February Harry is demobbed.
March William is demobbed.
May Cyril is demobbed.
June 1st Betty and Cyril are married.
July Bread rationed.

1947

June Eva marries Douglas, who she met at Betty and Cyril's wedding. Douglas was also a P.O.W..

1948

July Bread rationing ends.
December Jam rationing ends.

1952

October Tea rationing ends.

1953

February Sweet rationing ends.
April Cream rationing ends.
March Egg rationing ends.
September Sugar rationing ends.

1954

May Butter, cheese, margarine and cooking fat rationing ends.
June Meat rationing ends. No more rationing.

GLOSSARY

Anti-aircraft guns These were mobile guns which were fired at the German bomber aircraft as they flew over England. Known as Ack Ack, they were very noisy and the falling fragments of the shells they fired made them quite dangerous. Although they did not manage to destroy many enemy planes, they did help to keep them high in the sky (*see page 7*).

Axis Germany and Italy made an agreement in 1936. It was called the "Axis Pact" and formed the Berlin-Rome Axis. An axis is a central line around which something can rotate, and Mussolini claimed that European affairs rotated around Germany and Italy. Later, in 1936, both Germany and Italy made alliances with Japan, forming a Berlin-Rome-Tokyo Axis.

Barrage balloons The word "barrage" means an intensive attack using shells, bullets, bombs or other missiles. Barrage balloons (*see page 6*) were large balloons which were attached to the ground by ropes. They were floated over British cities to prevent low-level enemy bombers, especially the Stuka "dive-bomber" aircraft, from attacking them. Coloured silver and known as "blimps", they were wound up and down on their ropes by R.A.F. Balloon Command, which had sites in parks and other open spaces.

Black market During the war foodstuffs and clothing which had been stolen from warehouses or trains would sometimes be offered for sale illegally, in secret. They cost a lot of money, but the buyer did not have to hand over any coupons.

British Expeditionary Force (B.E.F.) The name of the British force sent to France at the start of the war (*see page 9*). In 1939 4 divisions of infantry soldiers were sent, and by May 1940 there were 10 infantry divisions and a tank brigade. They were commanded by Viscount Gort. By June 1940 the B.E.F. had been driven back to Dunkirk on the north coast of France, and had to be evacuated to England, leaving most of their weapons and tanks behind.

Censorship During the war, the Government prohibited British people from obtaining or communicating (by speaking or writing) any information which might be useful to the enemy. This meant that all letters going to and from servicemen overseas were read by censors, and anything which might help the enemy was blacked out so that it could not be seen. The Ministry of Information sent the B.B.C. (which was then the only radio station) and all the newspapers lists of subjects which they could not mention, including the positions of ships, army regiments and factories, and the latest developments in the invention of weapons.

Dictator An absolute ruler who uses force to impose and retain power.

Fascism A form of government which allows no other political parties to exist and is therefore opposed to democracy. It considers that the nation and race of which it is a part are more important than individual people. It keeps very tight control over the lives of the people it governs and is against liberal ideas such as freedom of speech. Benito Mussolini, (*see page 5*) who became dictator of Italy in 1925, developed the idea of Fascism.

Foster parent Someone who looks after a child as a parent, although he or she is not actually related to that child.

Girdle This is an elastic corset for women (*see page 16*). It covers the body from the waist to the tops of the legs, and is designed to make the wearer look slimmer.

Heavy Rescue Service This was made up of groups of civil defence workers known as "demolition squads". Their job was to go into bombed buildings, remove all the people (living or dead) that they could find, shift the rubble and tear down or shore up any existing walls to make the building safe (*see page 36*). Demolition squads were made up of men who had worked as bricklayers, plumbers and labourers before the war.

Lancaster bomber First flown in June 1941, this four-engine aircraft was the most successful British heavy bomber of the war, carrying up to 14,000 lb of bombs.

Larder A cupboard or room where food is stored, also called a pantry.

Lend-lease The American Government passed the "Lend-Lease" Act in March 1941, giving President Roosevelt power to send weapons to the Allies. Lend-lease agreements were made with both Great Britain and the Soviet Union, for weapons and other supplies to be bought on credit (*see page 4*).

Messerschmitt Designed by Willy Messerschmitt, this was the most famous German fighter aircraft of the war. The single-engine, single-seater *Me109* was very similar to the British Spitfire. There was also the *Me 110*, which had twin engines but was less successful in combat.

Ministry of Food This was one of a number of new ministries specially created to deal with the needs of the country during wartime. The job of the Ministry of Food was to organize rationing. It set up regional food offices which made sure that everyone in their region was given a ration book. The Ministry itself had divisions which were responsible for controlling the manufacture and distribution of different foods. For example, the Bacon and Ham Division gave farmers licences to keep pigs, bought all the meat that was produced and made sure that each butcher's shop got enough to supply the customers whose ration books were registered there (*see page 25*).

Nazism The political beliefs of the members of the National Socialist German Workers Party (shortened to Nazi), led by Hitler. Nazism was a form of Fascism, and Nazis believed that their leader should have absolute power, that all industry should be controlled by the state, and that there should be a "new order" (*see below*).

New Order Hitler's idea of a "new order" was based on his belief that Northern European "Aryan" people, especially Germans, were *ubermenschen* or supermen, and they should rule the world. Other races he called *untermenschen* or sub-humans, and he said they should be the slaves of the *ubermenschen*. He described Jewish people as Germany's enemies, and developed a plan called the "final solution", to kill them all. In order to kill as many as possible in the shortest time, he had concentration camps built and fitted with gas chambers for this purpose. Around six million Jewish people died in the camps, as well as many Poles, Russians, Gypsies and Germans who did not agree with Hitler's ideas.

Parachute Silk This was the material used for the canopies of parachutes. During the war it was in great demand for making clothes, and could often be obtained on the black market (*see above*).

Reprisal Weapons These were V-1 and V-2 bombs (*see page 7*). Altogether, 8,900 V-1s ("doodlebugs") were launched against Britain, destroying a total of 25,000 houses and killing 6,184 people, nearly all in London. People soon learned to recognize the sound made by the V-1 engines. If the sound stopped when the V-1 was above their heads, they took cover, because when the engine stopped, the flying bomb would fall to earth and explode. British fighter planes and anti-aircraft guns had to be careful not to shoot down the V-1s over towns or cities because of the damage they could cause when they fell. However, after a few months they were able to destroy 80% of them before they reached their targets. Against the V-2 rocket bombs, however, there was no known method of defence. A V-2 was twenty times more expensive to produce than a V-1. Only 1,115 were launched against Britain, but they succeeded in killing 2,754 people. The launch pads for the V-2s were in Northern France; they were captured by the Allies after the D-Day landings.

Sandbag A small sack which is filled with sand or soil and sealed. During the war sandbags were placed along the walls of buildings and around doorways to strengthen and protect them in case bombs fell nearby.

Spitfire British 8-gun single-seater fighter aircraft, designed in 1936 by Supermarine. At the time of the Battle of Britain, one-third of the R.A.F.'s single-seater fighter aircraft were Spitfires. These were a good match for Messerschmitts in aerial combat because they were fast and easy to manoeuvre. The older Hurricanes, which made up the other two-thirds of the R.A.F.'s single-seater planes, were not thought to be so successful as fighter aircraft.

Ultimatum A final condition which must be met within a given time. Chamberlain's ultimatum to Hitler on September 3rd 1939 was handed to the German government at 9am. It stated that if Hitler did not give the British government a promise that his troops would leave Poland by 11am, Britain would declare war on Germany. When the time ran out and no answer had been received, Britain declared war.

INDEX

PLACES TO VISIT

The following museums have displays on aspects of the Second World War:

MUSEUM OF ARMY FLYING
Middle Wallop, Stockbridge, Hampshire SO20 8DY
0264-384421

CABINET WAR ROOMS
Clive Steps, King Charles Street, London SW1 A 2AQ
0171-930 6961

CAERNARFON AIR WORLD
Air Caernarfon Ltd., Caernarfon Airport, Dinas, Dinlle, Caernarfon, Gwynedd LL54 5TP
01286-830800

CASTLE CORNET
St. Peter Port, Guernsey
01481-721657

COVENTRY CATHEDRAL
Pool Meadow, Coventry CV1 5ES
01203-227597

D-DAY MUSEUM AND OVERLORD EMBROIDERY
Clarence Esplanade, Portsmouth, Hampshire PO5 3NT
01705-827261

DOVER CASTLE AND HELLFIRE CORNER
Dover, Kent CT16 1HH
01304-201628

DUXFORD AIRFIELD (IMPERIAL WAR MUSEUM)
Duxford, Cambridge CB2 4QR
01223-835000

EDEN CAMP MODERN HISTORY THEME MUSEUM
Eden Camp, Malton, North Yorkshire YO17 0SD
01653-697777

FLEET AIR ARM MUSEUM
R.N.A.S. Yeovilton, Yeovil, Somerset BA22 8HT
01935-840565

HMS BELFAST
Morgans Lane, Tooley Street, London SE1 2JH
0171-407 6434

IMPERIAL WAR MUSEUM
Lambeth Road, London SE1 6HZ
0171-416 5000

MUSEUM OF LONDON
London Wall, London EC2Y 5HN
0171-600 3699

ROYAL AIR FORCE MUSEUM
Grahame Park Way, Hendon, London NW9 5LL
0181-205 2266

STATION 146
Stanmere, Seething, Norwich NR15 1AL
01508-550787 (essential to telephone before visiting)

TANGMERE MILITARY AVIATION MUSEUM
Tangmere Airfield, Tangmere, Chichester, West Sussex PO20 6ES
01243-775223

THE TANK MUSEUM
Bovington Camp, Nr. Wareham, Dorset BH20 6JG
01929-403463

WESTERN APPROACHES
123 Romford Street, Liverpool L2 3SZ
051-227 2008

THE WHITE CLIFFS EXPERIENCE
Market Square, Dover, Kent CT16 1PB
01304-214566

Acknowledgements

Black and white photographs © Imperial War Museum
p. 34-5 (centre) Courtesy of the Estate of Air Commodore N.C. Hyde

Breslich & Foss would like to thank Anita Ballin, Rachel Chinfen, Christopher Dowling, Jan Mihell and the Departments of Exhibits and Firearms, Printed Books, Documents, Design and Production, Art and Photographs of the Imperial War Museum, Jean Slee and June and William Wilson for their assistance.

We are especially grateful to the Allpress family and Cyril McCann for their help and patience.